# A
# DREAM
# COME TRUE

The
## STAINED GLASS WINDOWS
*of*
## ST. ANTHONY PARK
## LUTHERAN CHURCH,
## ST. PAUL, MINNESOTA

ANN STOUT

ISBN 1-880654-29-6.

Library of Congress Control Number 2003 106201

Book design and production by Mighty Media, Inc.
Interior design: Chris Long
Cover design: Kelly Doudna

Published by the Pogo Press, Incorporated.

# TABLE OF CONTENTS

# PREFACE

THE STAINED GLASS WINDOWS in the sanctuary of St. Anthony Park Lutheran Church represent a dream come true for a number of us in the congregation. Many people deserve special thanks. First, I would like to thank FLORENCE PREUS for the idea of having stained glass windows and for her faithful support through the process. Thanks go to PASTOR OFSTEDAL for his suggestions and contributions during the planning process and help with the text. Also, I am grateful to PASTOR GLENN BERG-MOBERG for his continuing support of a project which he did not begin. We are all so appreciative of NICHOLAS MARKELL, the artist who designed the windows, for his wonderful insights, theological knowledge, artistic vision, patience in working with our committee, and assistance with this written text.

Heartfelt thanks go to all of the members of the stained glass committee who gave of their time and knowledge: Jan Ansorge, Katherine Eklund (who helped in many ways), Wendell Frerichs (who helped especially with the Old Testament iconography), Fred Gaiser (for his knowledge of the Old Testament), Florence Preus, Maria Rogness, and Marvin Schindler (who also assisted with the photography and suggested the title).

I am grateful to Katherine Eklund, Jeanne Frerichs and Lois Anderson for their careful editing of the text. Thanks go to the church cabinet, past president, Blaine Thrasher, and present president, Jon Schumacher, for their continuing support of the stained glass window project. I humbly thank families of the congregation who saw fit to give money for the fabrication of the windows. St. Anthony Park Lutheran Church is also owed thanks for the Special Ministries Grant towards publication of this booklet. We thankfully acknowledge funds from the Alma Roisum Bequest for most of the publication costs.

Thanks are due to people who have answered my questions about their windows, specifically Connie Peterson of Incarnation Lutheran Church and Kathy Demars of the Basilica of St. Mary.

Finally I gratefully thank John Salisbury of Gaytee Glass Company and all of the staff, artists, craftsmen and women who have labored to construct and install the windows.

ANN STOUT, *chair*
Stained Glass Committee
March, 2003

# INTRODUCTION

S T. ANTHONY PARK LUTHERAN Church is located in the neighborhood of St. Anthony Park at 2323 Como Avenue West, St. Paul, Minnesota. St. Anthony Park is one of the historic neighborhoods in St. Paul. Farmers started arriving after the Minnesota Territory was established in 1849. By the 1870s land speculation was a popular activity in the area. One of the chief landowners of what was to become St. Anthony Park was William R. Marshall who thought the area would be a nice neighborhood for wealthy families who would like to live in between the two growing cities but not in them. After the incorporation of the St. Anthony Park Company in 1885, development proceeded not only in the platting of the area but in actual building of large and medium sized houses (Lanegran, 1–26). Churches followed soon after. The St. Anthony Park United Church of Christ was the first church built in the neighborhood, in 1887. By 1889 there was an Episcopalian church, and by 1891 the Methodists had their first building (Lanegran, 45–48). The century would turn before the Lutherans had their own place of worship.

In November, 2002, the congregation of St. Anthony Park Lutheran Church celebrated the centennial of its founding. It started its life as the Wartburg Evangelical Lutheran Congregation and was composed of the faculty, families, and students of the United Church Seminary, predecessor to Luther Seminary. The congregation worshipped in Wartburg Chapel at United Church Seminary. By the 1940s consensus was reached to build an independent church apart from the seminary. In 1947 Hills, Gilbertson and Hays of Minneapolis designed the new church for the congregation. Unfortunately, pledges did not meet the anticipated costs of building, and much of the project had to be scaled back. It was decided not to build a basement because of the unstable nature of the fill on the site. A planned bell tower on the corner of Luther Place and Como Avenue was set aside. The overall size and scale of the building was reduced. The Dean L. Wichter Company of Minneapolis broke ground April 25, 1948, and the church dedication took place on June 19, 1949 (Rutford et al. 4–10, 30–32).

The congregation undertook various building campaigns for alterations and expansions in 1954–56, in 1974, and during the 1980s and 1990s. An entirely new sanctuary was proposed for the congregation under the leadership of Elmer Andersen in the mid 1960s; however, this project was never realized (Rutford et al. 36–40). The most recent campaign which had an impact on the sanctuary began in 1999. Led by Glen Skovholt and Ann Stout, the congregation engaged SMSQ, an architectural firm located in Northfield which specializes in renovation of church buildings, and Langer Construction Company of St. Paul. Central to the remodeling project was the building of a windowed tower which would bring light into the interior of the sanctuary in order to create enough ambient light for stained glass windows. The tower would have another function deemed important to the building committee. With its cross atop the tower it would make our church more visible to the neighborhood and the casual passerby.

The six pairs of stained glass windows now completed on the Luther Place wall of St. Anthony Park Lutheran Church reflect years of planning, discussion, and prayer. In the early 1990s the congregation received a memorial gift designated for stained glass windows; other gifts followed, and soon a committee began the project, resulting in the windows you see now. Some of the mission goals of the congregation are partially satisfied by the stained glass windows. There was a desire to emphasize outreach in our ministry. There was also the feeling that our sanctuary needed to feel more welcoming. Some felt the large, white walls were sterile and that some kind of color was needed.

Nicholas Markell designed the windows with input from the stained glass committee, and the wise counsel of Pastor Paul Ofstedal. The committee has been committed to a window design that would be both beautiful and instructive and a strong statement of our corporate and individual faith. The artists and craftsmen and women of Gaytee Stained Glass in Minneapolis fabricated the windows.

# PASTORAL STATEMENTS

### PASTOR PAUL OFSTEDAL
*Former Pastor*

EVERY CHILD, INCLUDING THE CHILD IN EACH ONE OF us, loves a story. We especially need to know God's Great Salvation Story and that we are part of that story. Now our sanctuary, always a place for that Story verbally, is becoming also a visual wall-to-wall space for that Story.

In the Jewish roots of Christianity, which strictly warned against the idolatries of pagan neighbors, no religious images had been allowed. For the sake of children and the illiterate, the early church, in an ecumenical council at Nicaea, made a bold move. So that the Story might be better told, Jesus, biblical figures and Bible stories were allowed to be visually portrayed. Stained glass windows eventually became part of that effort.

Our beautiful stained glass windows are meant to tell the Bible Story. That's it! So I am thankful to have been among those who studied, explored, debated, and prayed for God's leading, that God's Great Salvation Story might be told in this place of worship, not for our ears alone, but also for our eyes.

## PASTOR GLENN BERG-MOBERG
*Present Pastor*

THE STAINED GLASS WINDOWS INCLUDE THE TREE of life as a repeating motif. You can see oak leaves and acorns that recall the old growth oak trees in our neighborhood. An acorn is a forward-looking item. Planting a slow-growing tree is a way of expressing a commitment to the future. Stained glass windows are like that. They may seem traditional, even old-fashioned. On the contrary, they are a gift to the future. The story of salvation, told in pictures, has been found by untold numbers of people to be a life-giving story. We hope and pray that here in this building people of the future will find life in Christ, and so become the fruit of this forward-looking gift.

## PASTOR LIN QIU
*Pastor of the Chinese Fellowship*

EVERY TIME THE SUNLIGHT PASSES THROUGH WINDOWS of our sanctuary, the stained glass pictures remind me that we, everyone who is in this place of worship, are in God's grace. The stained glass windows show us the main cores of the Bible: Creation, Salvation, and the New Heaven and Earth. The stained glass windows provide a visual way for those who have no Christian background to learn about God and His grace. The stained glass windows are not only wonderful art, but they are also an evangelical tool.

✺ ✺

# THE FABRICATION PROCESS

## The Artist

NICHOLAS MARKELL IS WELL KNOWN FOR HIS MANY creations in stained glass and painted icons in Minnesota and in several other states. He earned a Bachelor of Visual Arts degree at the University of St. Thomas in St. Paul but was always interested in the relationship between his artistic expression and spirituality. In 1987 he earned a Master of Arts degree in Theology and a Master of Divinity degree from the Washington Theological Union in Washington, D.C. He particularly enjoyed studying ancient Christian art and symbolism. Although he seriously considered ordination, Nicholas decided to run his own liturgical art company where he works in a variety of mediums. Nicholas' art reflects his deep understanding of religious thought. He has won many national awards and has exhibited his art in numerous shows, galleries, and academic institutions. He currently designs and illustrates books for several publishers. His original icons and stained glass windows can be found in over fifty churches across twenty states.

NICHOLAS MARKELL

## THE ARTIST'S STATEMENT

AS A LITURGICAL DESIGNER, I CREATE ART FOR WORSHIP. For the windows of St. Anthony Park Lutheran Church, whether I was focused on a person, event or belief, I was interested in spirituality. Indeed, my goal was not so much to create an image of what is *seen*, but rather what is *believed*. In doing this, I was called into a deeper life of Christian service, ever seeking a glimpse of the eternal in hopes of helping church members to explore more deeply the mystery and personal presence of God in their lives.

## THE ARTIST'S STUDIO

FOUNDED AFTER MANY YEARS OF PERSONAL EXPERI-
ence, education and professional work in art, theology
and ministry, **MARKELL STUDIOS** is dedicated to cre-
ating sacred art designed to serve the needs of churches
by laboring to create images of religious meaning, artistic
beauty, spiritual content and theological insight.

# The Glass Studio

GAYTEE STAINED GLASS, INC. OF MINNEAPOLIS FABricated the windows under the direction of the owner, John Salisbury. Gaytee was founded in 1918 by Thomas Gaytee. The company continues a tradition of fine craftsmanship in its studio today and is a highly respected stained glass fabricating and restoration company. Some of Gaytee's installations include windows by Nicholas Markell in the Cathedral Church of St. Mark, Minneapolis, the window by Michael Hope in the chapel of Central Lutheran Church, Minneapolis, the windows by Dan Johnson in Incarnation Lutheran Church in Shoreview, and the window by Dietrich Spahn at the First Presbyterian church in White Bear Lake. Gaytee also has worked extensively in buildings which are not churches. Some interesting examples include the Bobby Jones window designed by John Salisbury for the Interlachen Country Club, Minneapolis, the window by Richard Millard at the Lowell Inn in Stillwater, and windows currently being created by Rick Parlow and Michael Hope for the Royal Caribbean Cruise Line. Gaytee continues to do restoration of older windows as at the James J. Hill House in St. Paul and the Basilica of St. Mary in Minneapolis, where Thomas Gaytee designed the original windows.

# The Process

THE PROCESS OF MAKING STAINED GLASS IS EXCEED-
ingly time-consuming depending on age-old techniques
and handwork. After the design is finished the artist draws
a full-size cartoon of the entire window. The cartoon or
paper pattern contains all of the separate pieces made
up of the different colors. The colored glass needs to be
ordered. Decisions are made regarding color and texture.
Some of it has to be imported, but some is made in the

LARRY LINDQUIST

United States. An interesting blown glass imported from Germany, "Baroque glass," has bubbles in it. Other glass has swirls. Thus, in addition to many different colors, textures play a large part in the finished effect. Some glass is more opaque, and other glass is more clear, depending on the effect the artist wishes to achieve.

Once the glass is accumulated for the project, the cartoon is used to cut the different kinds of glass to the correct shapes. Details, such as fold lines, are hand painted on the individual glass pieces. After painting, the pieces of glass are put in a kiln and fired to between 1150 to 1200 degrees Fahrenheit to fix the paint onto the glass. The artist will also spend a considerable amount of time doing detailed hand painting of shadows. Each time more paint is added, the pieces are fired again. There could be as many as three firings. In putting the pieces together, each joint is soldered with lead strips. Then the work is flipped over, and the joints are soldered on the other side. Next there is a cementing process so that the piece will stay rigid. After cementing, the lead is burnished. Finally the stained glass is ready for installation.

In the case of our church we needed new frames to hold the glass. The frames accommodate not only the stained glass, but a second layer of clear glass for protection of the window and insulation against the extremes of weather.

SANCTUARY PRIOR TO INSTALLATION OF STAINED GLASS WINDOWS

# THE STAINED GLASS WINDOWS

## THE STYLE OF THE WINDOWS

THE CHURCH BUILDING IS IN THE GOTHIC STYLE WHICH ORIGI-nated in France in the twelfth century. Some of the hallmarks of the Gothic style include pointed arches, ribbed vaults, and large lancet windows (long and narrow with a pointed arch) filled with stained glass. This was a revolutionary style at the time. The previous style, called the Romanesque, had long barrel-vaulted ceilings, and usually much smaller windows. One goal of the Gothic style was to let in as much light as possible, especially colored light which would give the worshipper the feeling of entering the heavenly Jerusalem or a taste of heaven on earth. St. Anthony Park Lutheran Church has the pointed arches of the Gothic style. However, it lacks the ribbed vaults. Many churches in our modern age include some aspects of the Gothic style. The resulting compromise is called the Neo-Gothic style.

The committee liked the simplicity of the figure style of the Gothic period. On the one hand, the figures are simple and somewhat stylized; they hint of a spiritual and universal dimension beyond the stories. On the other hand, we have some historical accuracy, as in the simple shape of a plowshare or clay vessel, and contemporary elements, as in the Pentecost window, which shows all ages and races making up the church today.

Art in the Gothic period was very colorful, especially stained glass windows. Primary colors of red and blue were emphasized especially. The artist, Nicholas Markell, has chosen purposely to alternate the deep blue and turquoise windows throughout, to enliven the total composition.

# The Luther Place Side at a Glance

THE COMMITTEE WANTED A STAINED GLASS PROGRAM WHICH would encompass as many of the major messages of the Old and New Testaments as possible. Because the individual lancet windows are relatively small, 6 feet 6 inches by 20½ inches, some of the stories are implied through symbolic objects. Because of the limitations of money it was decided at the outset that the stained glass program would be limited to existing windows in the sanctuary. Thus although there was passing interest in a rose window, that circular window most representative of Gothic art, our building would not structurally allow for inclusion of a rose window, nor was it practical financially. Two of the windows have vents to allow for fresh air during the spring and fall. The vents were chosen where they would have a minimal impact on the design.

The windows proceed chronologically from left to right.

PAIR NUMBER ONE
*Creation* and *The Angels' Visitation to Abraham and Sarah*

PAIR NUMBER TWO
*Moses and the Exodus* and *The Prophets*

PAIR NUMBER THREE
*The Incarnation* and *The Epiphany*

PAIR NUMBER FOUR
*The Washing of the Feet* and *The Last Supper*

PAIR NUMBER FIVE
*The Deposition* and *The Resurrection*

PAIR NUMBER SIX
*Pentecost* and *The Heavenly Jerusalem*

SANCTUARY AFTER INSTALLATION OF STAINED GLASS WINDOWS

# The Luther Place Side:
## DESCRIPTION AND ICONOGRAPHY

### PAIR NUMBER ONE
*Creation* and *The Angels' Visitation to Abraham and Sarah*, plate 1.

LEFT. *The Creation*. Most striking is the eye of God within a trefoil (signifying the Trinity) at the peak of this window. The eye since ancient times has been a symbol of the all-seeing God; here the eye of God emerges from the darkness of chaos. The spirit of God swirls down toward a recognizable earth with the breath of God in Adam's nostrils. Eve appears from Adam's side (GENESIS 1:26, 27; 2:7–23). We see also spinning planets, stars, sun, life-giving water, doves, a jumping fish, and a tree with fruit.

In the small panel beneath the Creation window are the arc of a rainbow and a crescent, denoting God's promise not to flood the world again. We are reminded of how God rested after his work of creation and how we have the Sabbath rest, a time to bask in the beauty and goodness of creation.

RIGHT. *The Angels' Visitation to Abraham and Sarah*. In the pendant, or companion, window we see Abraham receiving the messengers of God humbly with a meal of bread and milk, likened to a sacrificial meal on an ancient altar and a suggestion of the Holy Meal to come. Often in Christian art winged people denote messengers. Abraham learns of God's plan for him and for his aged wife, Sarah: that they will have a child whose lineage will be blessed. Note the oak tree, the Tree of Life, and Sarah, in the tent, chuckling at this preposterous news! The altar has a hole in it. In the ancient world, the hole in an altar was a symbol of eternity.

In the small window beneath the Abraham and Sarah depiction are a dagger in the form of a cross (symbolizing the sacrifice of Isaac as told in GENESIS 22:1–13), a thicket (with thorns reminding us of the crown of thorns), and twelve stars, another promise for Abraham's descendants, who become the twelve tribes of Israel.

## PAIR NUMBER TWO
*Moses and the Exodus* and *The Prophets*, plate 2.

LEFT. *Moses and the Exodus.* In this powerful image, we view Moses, parting the Red Sea, but only with a reliance on God as the source of his powers; the crutch-staff, held high, signifies Moses' and our dependence on God (EXODUS 14:19–29). The pose of Moses, with his arms outstretched, looks forward to Christ's arms outstretched on the cross. The waters of the Red Sea remind us of the water of baptism. Again the oak seedling and acorn appear as symbols of life and hope even in devastation.

In the small window we find the burning bush in flames and God's word given to his messenger in the form of the Ten Commandments etched in stone.

RIGHT. *The Prophets.* The pendant window is highly symbolic, showing Nicholas Markell's depiction of the role of the prophets. A long scroll unfurls from the top of the window to the bottom with smaller scrolls unfurling horizontally. We see an image from MICAH 4:3, "and they shall beat their swords into plowshares." From other Old Testament books we see a fruiting tree: "Blessed is the man … who delights in the law of the Lord, and on His law he meditates day and night. He is like a tree planted by streams of water, that yields its fruit in its season, and its leaf does not wither," (PSALM 1:1–3). Lower down is a heart which is divided in half: "and I will take out of your flesh the heart of stone and give you a heart of flesh," (EZEKIEL 36:26). From the New Testament the Holy Spirit in the form of a dove is present at the baptism of Christ by John the Baptist, the last prophet (MATTHEW 3:13–17).

The shell is used to pour water for baptism, and the star symbolizes the prophets' profession of truth and light. The rising sun symbolizes Christ. Note the prophecy in MALACHI 4:2: "But unto you that fear my name shall the sun of righteousness arise with healing in his wings."

## PAIR NUMBER THREE
*The Incarnation* and *The Epiphany*, plate 3.

LEFT. *The Incarnation.* As told in LUKE 2:1–7, the Christ Child appears within a mandorla (an almond-shaped glory of light, which is also straw in the manger). The Child appears as not quite an infant but not as an adult, often seen in Gothic depictions of the Incarnation. Here the artist created a more universal Jesus, an image not easily dismissed or sentimentalized. In the Orthodox tradition, Christ's more adult face symbolized his divine wisdom. Behind His head is a halo or nimbus inscribed with a cross, which looks ahead to His suffering and death on the cross. The swaddling cloths remind us of the grave cloths. The ox, traditionally a sacrificial animal in the ancient world, foretells Christ's coming sacrifice on the cross. The ox and the ass were frequently shown in depictions of the Nativity in the early Christian period. They look lovingly at the Christ Child, recognizing him as the Savior. Behind the animals and Joseph's head is a cave. In the Orthodox church the traditional birthplace of Christ was a cave; then He was laid in a manger. In the western church the birthplace was a shed. The crib or crêche was introduced later with St. Francis. Note the bare feet of Jesus, symbolizing His humanity and humility. Mary is shown as a temple of the Holy Spirit with Christ still in her womb; her expression is that of the tender mother after the birth. The lamb at the feet of the Christ Child will appear again in glory in the sixth pair of windows. The star which guided the Magi on their journey rests now over the Holy Family.

The seraph or angel refers to the heavenly host rejoicing at the Savior's birth (LUKE 2:13, 14).

RIGHT. *The Epiphany.* The shepherds looking on symbolize the lowly (LUKE 2:15,17). The Magi are the foreigners. They are the ones who recognized the child as the Lord. They offer their gifts of gold, frankincense, and myrrh (MATTHEW 2:9–11). These precious objects refer to Christ as prophet, priest, and king. The gold relates to His kingship, as Lord of heaven and earth. The frankincense refers to His priestly role. The myrrh, used in the preparation of the dead, refers to His prophecy of His death.

The turtledoves refer to the Jewish law of sacrifice given when a new baby is presented at the temple. A wealthy family would offer a lamb, but a poor family could offer turtledoves (LUKE 2:23, 24).

## PAIR NUMBER FOUR

*The Washing of the Feet* and *The Last Supper* (JOHN 13:1–30), plate 4.

These are the only windows with a unified design field where the composition covers both lancet windows. We see Jesus as servant and Lord washing the feet of one of the disciples. He has a gold cross nimbus indicating His strength. In the Incarnation scene the cross nimbus was blue indicating His vulnerability. Only Christ has a cross nimbus, reminding us that He died on the cross for our sins. The young man to the left is John. John was traditionally depicted as the youngest disciple. He sits on a bench echoing the form of an altar, the table of sacrifice, which looks forward to the cross and reminds us that foot washing was a sacrificial act. John waits his turn, pointing to the bread (His body, given for us), and wine (His blood, shed for us). Judas, having betrayed Jesus, sneaks out into the night (its darkness symbolic of sin) with his bag of coins. The chalice can be interpreted as either a simple earthen jar with a golden glaze or as a chalice of gold; in either case, the gold symbolizes Christ's kingship. The four flames remind us of the four corners of the earth where the disciples would one day go with this good news.

The flames light up the interior of the Upper Room as the sun sets. The table breaks through the boundaries of the windows, hinting at eternity. The red carnation is a symbol of pure love.

## PAIR NUMBER FIVE
*The Deposition* and *The Resurrection*, plate 5.

LEFT. *The Deposition.* While Mary embraces the body of her son, Joseph of Arimathea, John the Evangelist, Nicodemus, and three women mourn the suffering and death of their Lord (JOHN 19:38, 39). The blue nimbus, matching that in the Incarnation window, shows Jesus as Lord but in His most vulnerable state as a human being, as infant and victim. The lightning bolt in the upper portion of the window reminds us of the rending of the curtain in the temple (MATTHEW 27:51). The setting is bleak, without a landscape but with the cross prominent, an allusion to the crucifixion just past.

In the lower window a Roman helmet, a spear which pierced Christ's side, and dice which were cast for His cloak are visible. They are symbols of the humiliation of Jesus at the hands of the Roman soldiers.

RIGHT. *The Resurrection.* Mary Magdalene mistakes the risen Christ for the gardener (JOHN 20:11–17). In the background are the tomb (echoing the cave of the *Incarnation*) and the Tree of Life. Together these images imply life emerging from death. We do not see the face of Christ, resurrected and in a new form. The vessel for the ointment is the same as the vessel in the *Epiphany* window.

Below is the food which Christ ate when He appeared to His disciples (LUKE 24:41, 42). In the ancient world eating food was a sign that someone was alive and not an illusion. The loaves and fish remind us of one of Christ's miracles, The Feeding of the Five Thousand.

## PAIR NUMBER SIX
*Pentecost* and *The Heavenly Jerusalem*, plate 6.

LEFT. *Pentecost.* In a reversal of the Tower of Babel we see human figures interweaving and forming a tower rising upward – men, women, and children working together to form the church. We are the church, rooted in the reality of Pentecost. The spirit of God begins in a flash of white and splits off into flames, becoming redder and more vibrant as it reaches into humanity (ACTS 2:1–4). The same swirling spirit of God is seen in the *Creation* window.

The symbol at the bottom is the world inscribed with a cross suggesting the great commission to preach the Gospel to all the world.

RIGHT. *The Heavenly Jerusalem.* Perhaps the most complex of all the windows is the *Heavenly Jerusalem* window. The imagery comes from the book of Revelation, which is rich in symbols and imagery. The Lamb of God is now seated on a jeweled throne with a cross nimbus, symbolic of the sacrificed and risen Christ. The River of Life flows through the heavenly Jerusalem, feeding the Tree of Life at the bottom of the window. The twelve jewels at each of the twelve gates form the foundation for the heavenly city (REVELATION 21:9–27). To the Israelites, heaven was the source of jewels. God's kingship was lowered from heaven. There are twelve windows on this wall. The jewel at the top of each signifies the twelve jewels of scripture, those found on the priestly garments and symbolic of the twelve tribes and the twelve apostles. They also remind us that our church participates in the faith of our ancestors and points to the glory which awaits us all in God's kingdom. The seven-pointed star denotes perfection, completion, and the seven gifts of the Holy Spirit.

The Tree of Life at the bottom is nourished by the River of Life (REVELATION 22:1, 2).

# The Luther Place Windows as Memorials

THE STAINED GLASS WINDOWS SERVE AS WONDERFUL MEMORIALS to family members of our congregation. Below are members memorialized as of this writing.

*The Creation* and *The Angel's Visitation to Abraham and Sarah*: in memory of Herman Preus.

*Moses and the Exodus* and *The Prophets*: in memory of Harriet Bestul.

*The Incarnation* and *The Epiphany*: in memory of Harold Arneman, Elaine Frost, Sigrid Harrisville, Thor Loney, F. W. "Woody" Thorstenson, and Allyn Thurow.

*The Washing of the Feet* and *The Last Supper*: in memory of Herman Preus

*The Deposition* and *The Resurrection*: in memory and honor of Joseph Skovholt and Elvera Skovholt.

*Pentecost* and *The Heavenly Jerusalem*: in memory of Christopher Stout.

# The Narthex Side at a Glance

THE WINDOWS ON THE NARTHEX SIDE ARE IN THE PROCESS OF fabrication. The stained glass committee wanted to include more imagery from the Life of Christ than was possible in the first six pairs of windows. The next five sets will include key scenes from the New Testament including miracles, parables, healings and scenes from the life of Christ. The final window pair will feature scenes from the life of the apostle Paul. Symbols at the bottom of the images will reflect the great "I am" statements of Jesus. The illustrations here are the artist's drawings.

The windows are described from left to right.

PAIR NUMBER ONE
*The Miracle of Turning Water into Wine at the Wedding at Cana* and *The Miracle of Loaves and Fishes*

PAIR NUMBER TWO
*The Prodigal Son* and *The Good Samaritan*

PAIR NUMBER THREE
*The Healing of the Paralytic* and *Christ as the Good Shepherd*

PAIR NUMBER FOUR
*The Conversion of Paul* and *Paul's Missionary Journeys*

PAIR NUMBER FIVE
*The Baptism of Christ* and *Christ with the Children*

# The Narthex Side:

## DESCRIPTION AND ICONOGRAPHY

**PAIR NUMBER ONE**
*The Miracle of Turning Water into Wine at the Wedding at Cana*
and *The Miracle of the Loaves and Fishes*, plate 7.

LEFT. *The Miracle of Turning Water into Wine at the Wedding at Cana*. This is the first miracle of Christ, the turning of water into wine found in JOHN 2:1–11. Christ is shown at His mother's urging in the act of turning the water into wine. Behind Christ and Mary is the newly married couple under the wedding canopy and a crown. Behind them is the father of the groom. It was customary at the time for the bride to go to the house of the groom's father. The whole scene can be compared to a foreshadowing of the heavenly banquet. We are also reminded of Jesus' words describing heaven: "In my father's house there are many rooms," (JOHN 14:2).

At the bottom a grape vine wraps around a cross symbolizing Jesus' words from JOHN 15:1–2, "I am the true vine, and my father is the vine dresser. Every branch of mine that bears no fruit, he takes away, and every branch that does bear fruit he prunes, that it may bear more fruit."

RIGHT. *The Miracle of Loaves and Fishes*. Another name for this miracle is the Feeding of the Five Thousand (MARK 6:35–44 and JOHN 6:1–14). A young boy offers Jesus his basket of fish while Jesus holds up the five loaves. The crowd is behind under a tree signifying the Tree of Life. Christ holds two loaves in one hand symbolizing the two natures of Christ. He is true God and true man. In the other hand He holds three loaves symbolizing the trinity. He is looking up towards the heavens to His heavenly father.

A sheaf of wheat symbolizes the saying "I am the bread of life; he who comes to me shall not hunger," (JOHN 6:35).

**PAIR NUMBER TWO**
*The Prodigal Son* and *The Good Samaritan*, plate 8.

LEFT. *The Prodigal Son.* This parable comes from LUKE 15:11–24. The son is bent down with remorse, wearing nothing but a coarse blanket. Tears of repentance flow down his cheeks. His father embraces him tenderly in forgiveness. Behind them stands the faithful but angry brother who stayed home. To the side is the fatted calf the father has ordered to be used for the homecoming celebration. At the rear is the great house of the father symbolizing the heavenly Jerusalem, or the home of God, our Father in heaven.

A many-pointed star reminds us of the words of Jesus in REVELATION 22:16, "I am the root and the offspring of David, the bright morning star."

RIGHT. *The Good Samaritan.* This parable comes from LUKE 10: 30–37. The good Samaritan has placed the stripped and beaten man on his own beast and is taking him to an innkeeper. In the background are the priest and the Levite who turned their backs on the injured man.

A lamb with a shepherd's crook refers to the words in JOHN 10: 14, "I am the good shepherd; I know my own and my own know me."

## PAIR NUMBER THREE
*The Healing of the Paralytic* and *Christ as the Good Shepherd*, plate 9.

LEFT. *The Healing of the Paralytic.* This is a dramatic scene with the paralyzed man lowered down through the roof because of the press of people. This scene underscores the faith of the whole community where many people worked together to get the paralyzed man into the presence of Jesus and his healing (MARK 2:1–5). Today we are reminded of what we can do as a congregation when we all work together.

The interwoven letters A and O come from REVELATION 1:8, "I am the Alpha and Omega, says the Lord God, who is and who was and who is to come, the Almighty."

RIGHT. *Christ as the Good Shepherd.* Here we see Christ as our personal and comforting Good Shepherd of the Twenty-third Psalm: "The Lord is my shepherd, I shall not want; he makes me lie down in green pastures. He leads me beside still waters; he restores my soul." The mountains and lake behind reflect the beauty of creation.

An open book with a cross over it and the barely visible Tree of Life behind it shows the word of God, the Bible. Here the word is also Christ, "In the beginning was the Word, and the Word was with God, and the Word was God," (JOHN 1:1).

## PAIR NUMBER FOUR

*The Conversion of Paul* and *Paul's Missionary Journeys*, plate 10.

LEFT. *The Conversion of Paul.* Saul (his name before his conversion) is on his way to Damascus when he has a life-shaking experience (ACTS 9:1–9). He is blinded by great beams of light which stream down, an encounter with the living God. He is visibly shaken. Even his garments seem to move. He drops his sword and two stones. The stones refer to Saul's presence and complicity at the stoning of Stephen, the first Christian martyr. The sword was the instrument of the persecution which Saul meant to carry out against Christians in Damascus, but it eventually becomes a symbol of his own martyrdom. Damascus is in the distance. It will be a kind of heavenly Jerusalem for Saul where he will start his new life as Paul.

The symbol is a flaming sun for Jesus' saying from JOHN 9:5, "as long as I am in the world, I am the light of the world."

RIGHT. *Paul's Missionary Journeys.* The window opposite Paul's conversion is symbolic like the *Prophets* window on the other side of the sanctuary. A ship and stormy sea recall the dangers of his missionary voyages. The pots remind us of Paul's words, "we have this treasure in earthen vessels, to show that the transcendent power belongs to God and not to us," (2 CORINTHIANS 4: 7). The cross symbolizes the cross of Christ crucified, which Paul preached to the Gentiles. Note that the design of the cross looks like our own new crosses in the sanctuary and atop the cupola. The Parthenon symbolizes Paul's preaching in cities such as Athens. The Holy Spirit flame symbolizes the inspiration for his work and writing and Paul's passion for his mission. The chains symbolize his imprisonment for the faith. The scroll points to his epistles. Finally, the purple cloth symbolizes the work of Lydia, an important woman in the early church who was a dyer of cloth. Early ministry was a cooperative effort including many women. Moreover, purple was the color of royalty and the Roman imperial family and thus especially suitable for the son of God.

## PAIR NUMBER FIVE

*Christ and the Children* and *The Baptism of Christ,* plate 11. The fifth pair frames the new entry door into the sanctuary.

LEFT. *Christ and the Children.* This grouping shows children of different ages including one who is lame, bolstering the idea of healing. The window is meant to encourage the children of the congregation and recalls a saying of Jesus, "Let the children come to me and do not hinder them; for to such belongs the kingdom of God," (MARK 10:14).

The torch is an alternative symbol for Christ as the light of the world and also represents knowledge. Here it refers to Christ as teacher and nurturer of children.

RIGHT. *The Baptism of Christ.* Christ is being baptized by John the Baptist at the Jordan River. This window emphasizes the sacrament of baptism. It is fitting that it is opposite the sacrament of Holy Communion depicted on the north wall. John pours water on Jesus' head while the Holy Spirit dove alights on Jesus' head, (MATTHEW 3:13–17).

The white lily symbolizes another saying of Jesus, "I am the resurrection and the life; he who believes in me, though he die, yet shall he live, and whoever lives and believes in me shall never die," (JOHN 11:25–26).

# The Narthex Windows as Memorials

These are the narthex windows pledged at this writing:

*The Miracle of Turning Water into Wine at the Wedding at Cana* and *The Miracle of Loaves and Fishes*: In memory of Howard W. Lindgren by Martha Lindgren; in memory of Edgar and Myrtle Larson by Wendell and Jeanne Frerichs; given by Marvin and Ellen Schindler; in thanks to God from Sieg and Ann Rabie; in memory of Alfred Nier; from Kent and Katherine Eklund in gratitude for our faith community.

*The Prodigal Son* and *The Good Samaritan*: in the name of the Trovatten family.

*The Healing of the Paralytic* and *Christ as the Good Shepherd*: to the glory of God from Elizabeth and Frederick Morlock.

*The Conversion of Paul* and *Paul's Missionary Journeys*: in the name of the Teeter family.

*The Baptism of Christ* and *Christ and the Children*: in memory of John Tracy Anderson.

# FURTHER READING

*The Holy Bible*, Revised Standard Version.

Brown, Sarah. *Stained Glass: an Illustrated History*. London: Bracken Books, 1994.

Ferguson, George. *Signs and Symbols in Christian Art*. New York, NY: Oxford University Press, 1961.

Lanegran, David A. *St. Anthony Park: Portrait of a Community*. St. Paul, MN: St. Anthony Park Community Council and St. Anthony Park Association, 1991.

Rutford, John, Mary Mergenthal, David Hansen, Lois Anderson, eds. *One Hundred Years of Lutheran Ministry in St. Anthony Park, St. Paul, Minnesota, 1902–2002*, 2002.

Sill, Gertrude Grace. *A Handbook of Symbols in Christian Art*. New York, NY: Macmillan Publishing Co. Inc., 1975.

# LIST OF ILLUSTRATIONS

**PHOTOGRAPHS**

Except as indicated, all photographs were taken by Ann Stout.

**FRONT COVER**
*The Last Supper* and *The Washing of the Feet*.

**BACK COVER**
St. Anthony Park Lutheran Church, St. Paul, Minnesota.

**PAGE 9**
Nicholas Markell, the artist, in the Gaytee studio. Photograph by John Salisbury.

**PAGE 10**
John Salisbury, owner, Gaytee Stained Glass, Inc., selecting glass for the project.

**PAGE 12**
Larry Lindquist, foreman of the Gaytee studio, examines a piece of glass for the cartoon.

**PAGE 14**
St. Anthony Park Lutheran Church sanctuary before installation of stained glass windows.

**PAGE 17**
St. Anthony Park Lutheran Church sanctuary after installation of stained glass windows.

**PAGE 47**
The author, Ann Stout, in front of the St. Anthony Park Lutheran Church. Photograph by Pastor Reany Lindberg.

# PLATES (PAGES 18–41)

PLATE 1

PAIR NUMBER ONE: *The Creation* and *The Angels' Visitation to Abraham and Sarah.*

PLATE 2

PAIR NUMBER TWO: *Moses and the Exodus* and *The Prophets.*

PLATE 3

PAIR NUMBER THREE: *The Incarnation* and *The Epiphany.*

PLATE 4

PAIR NUMBER FOUR: *The Washing of the Feet* and *The Last Supper.*

PLATE 5

PAIR NUMBER FIVE: *The Deposition* and *The Resurrection.*

PLATE 6

PAIR NUMBER SIX: *Pentecost* and *The Heavenly Jerusalem.*

The following images are Nicholas Markell's original drawings for the narthex side:

PLATE 7

PAIR NUMBER ONE: *The Miracle of Turning Water into Wine at the Wedding at Cana* and *The Miracle of Loaves and Fishes.*

PLATE 8

PAIR NUMBER TWO: *The Prodigal Son* and *The Good Samaritan.*

PLATE 9

PAIR NUMBER THREE: *The Healing of the Paralytic* and *Christ as the Good Shepherd.*

PLATE 10

PAIR NUMBER FOUR: *The Conversion of Paul* and *Paul's Missionary Journeys.*

PLATE 11

PAIR NUMBER FIVE: *Christ and the Children* and *The Baptism of Christ.*

# ABOUT THE AUTHOR

ANN STOUT HAS LIVED IN ST. ANTHONY PARK WITH HER husband, Jim, for thirty-one years. A native of California, she began her undergraduate education at the University of California, Berkeley, and finished it at the University of Alaska, Fairbanks. After a period of time as a studio potter, Ann had a strong desire to return to school in Art History. She earned her M.A. in 1981 and her Ph.D. in 1985. Since completing her degrees she has taught art history in small, private liberal arts colleges in the Twin Cities and greater Minnesota, including Hamline University, Macalester College, St. John's University, Gustavus Adolphus College, St. Olaf College, and Normandale Community College. She presently teaches art history at the College of Visual Arts in St. Paul. Ann has been active in St. Anthony Park Lutheran Church for about twenty-five years, serving on various commissions, as vice president of the congregation, as a Sunday school teacher, as co-chair of the building committee during the last renovation, and as chair of the stained glass window committee.